Everything You Need to Know About

Racism

An Introduction for Teens

Understanding racism begins by examining our own attitudes and prejudices towards others.

Everything You Need to Know About **Racism**

An Introduction for Teens

Nasoan Sheftel-Gomes

305.8
SHEf

The Rosen Publishing Group, Inc.
New York

To my grandparents, for their love. To my parents, for teaching me to be open-minded and for supporting me in everything I do. To Aumijo, for listening.

Special thanks to Cassius Gil's 9th- and 10th-grade classes at Fannie Lou Hamer Freedom High School, Bronx, NY, and Alex Milton's students at the Little Red Schoolhouse in New York City.

Published in 1998, 2000 by The Rosen Publishing Group, Inc.
29 East 21st Street, New York, NY 10010

Library of Congress Cataloging-in-Publication Data

Sheftel-Gomes, Nasoan.
    Everything you need to know about racism/Nasoan Sheftel-Gomes.- Revised ed.
       p. cm.
    Includes bibliographical references and index.
    Summary: Discusses the nature and effects of racism and ways to deal with it and take a stand against it.
    ISBN: 0-8239-3279-6
    1. Racism—United States—Juvenile literature. 2. Social conflict—United States—Juvenile literature. 3. United States—Race relations—Juvenile literature. [1. Racism. 2. Race relations. 3. Prejudice.] I. Title.
E184.A1S574 1998
305.8'00973—dc2

                                       98-11390
                                       CIP
                                       AC

Contents

Introduction

Gloria is a first-generation Cuban. When she won a scholarship to attend a top private school, her parents were proud. Neither of them had ever gone to school. Gloria felt strange leaving her old school, where most of the kids were Hispanic, to go to a place where everyone was white. Even though she felt strange at her new school, she made friends quickly.

After school, Gloria often hung out at her friends' houses. Lately, however, she felt uncomfortable whenever she went to Alexa's house. She had a feeling that Alexa's mom did not like her. When Alexa's other friends came over, Mrs. Forest kissed them and chatted away, but she barely said hello to Gloria. Gloria didn't know what to do. Everyone thought Mrs. Forest was the coolest mom, so Gloria couldn't complain to anyone. She felt that Mrs. Forest did not like her because she was a dark-skinned Latina.

As Gloria was discovering, racism is a tricky thing. It is much more than insulting someone based on his or her color, nationality, or religion. Racism can rear its ugly head in many ways, some of which are obvious, such as name-calling or telling racist jokes. Other ways can be much subtler. If a black woman and a white woman—both equally qualified—compete for the same job, and the white woman is hired, was the black woman a victim of discrimination? Sometimes you may feel that you are being discriminated against but not have any proof. Subtle forms of discrimination like this show how complicated an issue racism is.

You have probably grown up seeing images of racial conflict on television. Perhaps you remember the story of Rodney King, the black motorist who was beaten by four white Los Angeles policemen. Although the beating was videotaped, the four white policemen were judged innocent in court. Such injustice resulted in outraged black citizens taking to the streets in a series of riots that spread throughout several American cities.

More recently, the 1999 police shooting of African immigrant Amadou Diallo in New York City ignited new racial conflict. Even though the four police officers involved were indicted for second-degree murder, the event sparked angry protests around the country. These are two extreme examples of racial prejudice and hatred in the United States, but they are not the most common ones.

As in Gloria's case, racism can be difficult to identify. You may feel its effects but not be able to describe it to others. For a long time, racism in the United States was clearly visible. In a very obvious way, black Americans had fewer rights and fewer opportunities than white Americans. In fact, by law, blacks could not vote, own property, or live and go to school where they wanted. Such freedoms were kept from blacks by segregation laws. If blacks did not obey these discriminating laws, they risked violence and punishment.

It was only as recently as the 1960s that the civil rights movement changed this situation. Civil rights laws assured equal rights not only for blacks, but for all minorities. Now it does not matter what color you are or what race, religion, or ethnic group you belong to. All Americans can vote, live where they want, and go to school where they please. At the same time, however, laws cannot control every kind of racism. The much more frequent, subtler kinds of discrimination, as well as explosive, violent kinds, still exist.

All ethnic groups—from Mexican American and Native American to African American and Asian American—have experienced the painful reality of being viewed and treated as "the other" or "the outsider" in our society. As a result, these groups all share a common experience. Throughout U.S. history, they have had to struggle to be accepted and respected. Strangely enough, however, instead of feeling united by their problems, individuals of some ethnic groups end up discriminating against each other. Treating others with the same prejudices that you or your ethnic group has experienced is not only sad, it is hypocritical.

One of the keys to getting rid of racism is to change ignorant attitudes that you or someone you know may have. The difficulty is that many people cannot see that they have racist opinions. Because "racism" is such an ugly word, it is hard to take an honest look at yourself and admit to being prejudiced.

Another way of breaking down prejudices is to learn about other cultures and traditions. Many racist opinions and stereotypes come from ignorance and fear of the unknown. Once someone or something becomes familiar, it is no longer a threat.

In the end, we all need to recognize that our future is dependent on how we treat each other as individuals. Frederick Douglass, former slave, abolitionist, and author, once said, "The destiny of the colored American. . . is the destiny of America."

Whether we are black or white or of any other race, we are all Americans, and as Americans we are dependent on each other to move forward as a nation. As part of the next generation, you, too, can help make a difference in the fight against racism.

Christopher Columbus was said to have discovered America when in fact it was already inhabited by Native peoples.

Chapter One | A Brief History of Racism in the United States

Racism is the belief that one race of people is better than all others. It is the idea that a person's worth and ability are based on his or her race. Racism is also the hostility that some people feel for each other because of their different races. By understanding the roots of racism, you will be better able to understand how racism affects you—whatever your race may be.

"Discovering" America

In August 1492, the explorer Christopher Columbus set sail with three ships toward what he thought was Asia in search of the "riches of the Orient." Instead, Columbus "discovered" America on October 12, 1492, when he caught sight of the Bahamas. The natives, the Arawak Indians, swam from shore to greet him. Columbus took these native peoples aboard his ships as slaves and insisted they show him where to find the gold he had promised the king and queen of Spain, who had sponsored the trip.

In 1494, on a second trip, Columbus again traveled to the Caribbean in search of gold. After finding none, Columbus and his men imprisoned more than 11,000 Arawak men, women, and children; they even tried to take 500 of them back to Spain. Two hundred died during the journey. Those who remained were forced to search for gold. If they did not find any they were tortured—their hands were cut off and they were left to bleed to death. In two years, half of the 250,000 Indians on what is now Haiti were dead.

Slave Labor

By the early 1800s, nearly four million black slaves lived and worked in the United States. Many of them were shipped there after being stolen or sold in their native Africa. Those who survived the dangerous trip by boat were sold or auctioned off to white plantation owners, who used the Africans to work their fields, serve their families, and clean their houses.

The African slaves were treated as badly as and sometimes worse than the farmers' animals. They were beaten, whipped, tortured, and made to work long hours in the fields for no pay. Slave owners could do what they pleased with their slaves—even kill them—and it was not against the law. Slave owners destroyed families by separating mothers from

Slave owners forced many Africans into a life of slavery.

children and husbands from wives. Many slaves tried to run away and find their family members, but this was punishable by harsh laws.

In 1850 the Fugitive Slave Act was passed. The act made it easy for slave owners to recapture slaves who had escaped to the North or simply to pick up blacks they said had escaped. During the early 1800s, one thousand slaves a year escaped to the North, where blacks were free from slavery but not necessarily free from racism. Many of the slaves who made it to the North had the help of free blacks who risked their lives to help them escape and northern white abolitionists who did not believe in slavery.

Slavery was abolished when the Civil War ended.

The Underground Railroad

Harriet Tubman was born into slavery. She managed to escape and became the most famous conductor on the Underground Railroad—a network of houses and other places organized by free blacks and sympathetic whites to help slaves escape. The Underground Railroad helped thousands of slaves to freedom. Harriet Tubman herself made 199 dangerous trips back and forth, helping more than three hundred slaves to freedom.

During this period, the U. S. economy and land holdings continued to expand. This growth was achieved by the use of black slave labor and the purchases of land from

European countries. Furthermore, white pioneers moved farther west, claiming land as they went. Native Americans were considered obstacles in the path of westward expansion. They were forced off their land and either went west or fought, and most often died, for their land.

The Civil War (1861–1865)

The Civil War began in 1861, the year following the election of President Abraham Lincoln, who opposed the spread of slavery. Eleven southern states (the Confederacy) seceded, or separated, from the North (the Union). Southerners believed that President Lincoln wanted to change their way of life, including slavery, and they fought the northerners who supported him. Slavery was a central issue in the Civil War. The Confederacy wanted to maintain slavery whereas the Union wanted to abolish it.

In an attempt to get the southern states to reenter the Union, President Lincoln issued the Emancipation Proclamation on January 1, 1863. It was meant to punish the southern states that continued to fight against the Union. In hopes of preserving the Union, the Proclamation said that slaves in those southern states that continued to fight against the North were free. However, the Proclamation did not free the slaves who lived in states that remained a part of the Union.

After Reconstruction, southern states enacted segregation laws. Blacks were forced to use separate, often inferior, facilities.

Reconstruction (1865–1877)

When slavery was abolished in 1865, blacks enjoyed a temporary improvement in their quality of life during the post–Civil War period called Reconstruction. However, many were still poor and uneducated. Reconstruction was a period of hope when blacks were able to vote, hold political office, and start schools. During Reconstruction, blacks were divided about what rights to pursue now that they were free. Blacks had more opportunities than ever before, but some whites were becoming nervous about sharing their power.

In 1877, Reconstruction ended and violence and terror erupted in the South. Beatings, murders, and race riots became common, and many blacks were killed.

Much of the violence came from the Ku Klux Klan (KKK), a terrorist group in the South that formed in 1866 and whose members believed in white supremacy. Men in the KKK wore white sheets and burned crosses in the yards of black people's homes. Many blacks were lynched by these angry mobs of hooded men. These attacks were used to keep blacks from voting through fear and intimidation.

Segregation Laws

In the twentieth century, more and more blacks moved to the North in search of better lives. However, even in the northern cities, segregation existed in housing and schools. In the 1896 Supreme Court case called *Plessy vs. Ferguson*, the court ruled that having separate but equal schools, transportation, and housing for blacks and whites was legal. Therefore, segregation was legal.

In the South, Jim Crow laws were developed to make sure blacks and whites lived separately. These laws kept blacks and whites segregated from one another as much as possible and kept blacks poor and without power. Blacks were forced to use separate water fountains labeled "colored," and they were forced to sit at the back of the bus and to give up their seats if a white person was standing. They were not allowed in some places at all. Black schools were not as good as white

From 1820 to 1930, many immigrants came through Ellis Island, off the coast of New York City, pictured here.

schools, and living conditions for blacks were bad. What blacks had was separate, but it was not equal.

Immigrants

Racism did not affect only blacks and Native Americans. During this time, immigrants were pouring into North America from all over Europe. They were mostly poor, and many were without anything when they arrived. Some, like the Jewish immigrants, were fleeing persecution in their own countries. The huge numbers of immigrants looking for work kept wages low (because they would work for little pay) and, as a result, many suffered from poor working conditions.

Even though the United States is made up of immigrants, the new immigrants were looked down upon in their new home. Racism existed between immigrant groups because there was so much competition for the few opportunities that were available. For example, many Irish immigrants who had been in America for a while resented the new Jewish immigrants moving into their neighborhoods. In one incident in 1902 in New York, a large Jewish funeral for an important rabbi was attacked by an angry mob of Irish people. The police force was mostly Irish at that time, and an official investigation proved that Irish policemen helped the rioters.

By 1880 there were 75,000 Chinese immigrants in California. They had been brought in by the railroad companies to do the difficult work of building rail-roads. The Chinese immigrants were segregated from whites in schools and were not allowed to vote. They were subjected to continual violence. Many laws were created to keep the Chinese from having equal opportunities. The Chinese Exclusion Act of 1882 prohibited more Chinese laborers from entering the country. Later, during World War II, both American and Canadian governments forced Japanese citizens and their North American–born offspring (more than 120,000 people in the United States alone) into internment camps. Although most were completely innocent, several years passed before they were all allowed to return home. Even worse, many returned to houses that had been robbed, damaged, or destroyed.

Undeniably, the roots of racism run deep in the United States. Fighting racism has always been a difficult struggle, and it is one that continues to this day. The next chapter will discuss some of the important events and people of the civil rights movement.

Chapter Two | The Civil Rights Movement

The National Association for the Advancement of Colored People (NAACP), founded in 1909, fought many civil rights battles. The NAACP's most notable victory was the landmark decision of the Supreme Court in *Brown vs. Board of Education.* On May 17, 1954, the Supreme Court ruled unanimously that segregated schools were unconstitutional. On September 5, 1957, nine black students (the "Little Rock Nine") reported for school at Central High School in Little Rock, Arkansas. Because of television, people saw the fight that some white Arkansans waged to keep their schools all white.

The nine students were met by a mob of whites who were determined to keep schools separate. The white protesters screamed ugly names. The students were turned away at the door of the school. Two weeks later, President Dwight Eisenhower had federal troops escort

Rosa Parks's refusal to give up her seat on a public bus sparked the Montgomery bus boycott.

the black students into school. The students finally succeeded in getting an equal education. Meanwhile, the civil rights movement was taking shape, and distinctive leaders were emerging.

Rosa Parks

On December 1, 1955, Rosa Parks got on a bus to go home. When a white passenger got on, the bus driver ordered her to give up her seat. Mrs. Parks refused, was arrested, and thrown in jail. The black people of Montgomery, Alabama, decided to take action. Mrs. Parks filed a lawsuit, and the blacks boycotted the buses. Dr. Martin Luther King Jr., a young minister at the local church, became the leader of the Montgomery bus boycott. After thirteen months, the laws were changed, and blacks were allowed to sit where they wanted—first come, first served. It was another major victory in the fight for equal rights.

Dr. Martin Luther King Jr.

Dr. Martin Luther King Jr. became a great leader in the civil rights movement. Known for his belief in peaceful protest, he helped black Americans move toward equality before he was assassinated in 1968. Dr. King's strategy of nonviolent protest won him the support of black *and* white northerners. In 1963, he organized a march on Washington and delivered his "I Have a Dream" speech.

Because of King's work, President Kennedy supported a ban on discrimination. Many of the antidiscrimination laws that were passed, such as the Voting Rights Act of 1965, came into effect during President Lyndon Johnson's term.

Malcolm X

The black power movement, started by young blacks who wanted the same opportunities as whites, had its heyday in the late 1960s and early 1970s. Members of the movement felt that peaceful protests were not getting them anywhere. One of their leaders, Malcolm X—a Muslim minister when he became a prominent leader—believed that blacks should gain their rights "by any means necessary." He later became less militant. He thought that blacks could rely only on themselves for equality. In 1965, Malcolm X was assassinated while making a speech in New York.

Thousands of blacks and whites fought for civil rights in the 1960s. People were shocked by televised images of peaceful protesters being attacked by dogs. Aside from Martin Luther King Jr., Rosa Parks, and Malcolm X, there were other people who made a difference, including students whose "sit-ins" at segregated lunch counters allowed people of all races to eat together. The tragic and senseless death of Emmet Till, a fourteen-year-old black boy from Chicago who was murdered because he spoke to a white woman, forced people to do something about the evils of racism.

Malcolm X promoted brotherhood between blacks and whites.

By the end of the 1960s, many changes had occurred in the United States, such as the establishment of the affirmative action policy. It was designed to increase the proportion of minorities in the workplace and in schools long dominated by whites. In general, the policy requires employers and institutions to set goals for hiring or admitting members of minority groups.

Opponents of affirmative action say it is "reverse discrimination," favoring one group over another in a "nondemocratic" way. The 1990s have seen a backlash against affirmative action, some of which comes from white men who think that this policy robs them of jobs. However, a growing number of minorities say the benefits are countered by the belief that what they achieve is based on their color or gender instead of their talent.

President Clinton strongly defends affirmative action and feels that the fight against discrimination is not over. However, recent Supreme Court decisions have limited it considerably. Some states, such as California (which passed an initiative to do away with sexual and racial preferences), have adopted anti–affirmative action positions. Meanwhile, schools, universities, and workplaces across the United States continue to debate affirmative action's usefulness. One thing is certain, however: Race continues to be a complex issue, and despite many victories, the battle against prejudice still needs to be fought.

Chapter Three

Racism in Your Life

Because racism today reveals itself in ways that are often less directly in-your-face, it is often more difficult to detect—and more difficult to confront. Remember, in the introduction, how confused Gloria felt about the way Alexa's mom was treating her? This chapter will explore many different stereotypes and prejudices that are common today. It is these negative stereotypes—and the ignorance that keeps them alive—that allow racism to continue to thrive.

Livia was nervous about her interview for one of the top advertising agencies in the country. As she took the elevator to the top floor, she checked her lipstick in the mirror, straightened her new skirt, and told herself to stay cool. When the elevator doors opened, Livia was in the lobby of a penthouse office. Feeling jittery, she stepped toward the reception desk, where the receptionist —a young Hispanic woman such as herself—shot her what she took to be a friendly look.

"I'm Livia Gonçalez," Livia announced. "I'm here about the summer internship."

"Sorry, hon," said the receptionist. "You're out of luck. They just hired my replacement this morning."

Livia stood there stunned while the receptionist filed her nails. Livia felt stupid. Then annoyed. Why did this woman assume that she was here for a receptionist's job? Just because she was Hispanic, too? The receptionist finally looked up at Livia and with an impatient sigh said, "Look, I told you, the position is filled."

Livia wanted to yell, but she forced herself to be cool and professional. "I'm sorry, I didn't make myself clear. I'm here for the editorial internship."

Livia's story shows how people are often mistakenly judged by the way they look—even by people of their own race or background. Dark-haired and dark-skinned Livia was applying for a job in a firm where the majority of the employees were white. It thus seemed natural to the receptionist that a Latina such as herself would be applying for an internship as a receptionist instead of that as an editor. This kind of misunderstanding may not seem like a big deal, but if it occurs repeatedly, it can make you feel self-conscious. Livia was able to overcome her anger and act in a calm and professional manner. But not everybody can overcome the negative impacts of stereotyping every time it occurs.

Most white people living in North America never even think twice about their race. Usually, the only time whites might think about their "whiteness" is when they find themselves in a room, a part of town, or a foreign country in which they are the minority. Even under such circumstances, a white person is probably thinking more about the other people's race than his or her own.

Meanwhile, even in your own country, city, or neighborhood, if you are a nonwhite, you may be judged or singled out each time you walk down the street, enter a store, or eat at a restaurant. Furthermore, even when you are reading a magazine, are at the movies, or are watching television, it might bother you to note that images of your race are unfair, simplistic, or negative. Often your race might not be shown at all.

Stereotypes

It is easy to forget that each person is unique. If people weren't so quick to judge, we wouldn't hear prejudiced statements like, "Black people are dangerous" or "Mexicans are lazy" or "White people think they know everything." These statements are based on stereotypes. A stereotype is an unfair assumption formed when the actions of one person become the basis for judging a whole group of people. Stereotypes are usually negative and based on ignorance.

The Media

Stereotypes are often found in the media—television, movies, newspapers, magazines, radio, and even the Internet. The media has the power to influence many people. Unfortunately, the media can also promote negative stereotypes. When you watch television or go to a movie, you often see characters portrayed in a way that does not present a complete or honest picture. For example, if you were to watch a whole week's worth of prime-time television, you might notice that the criminals are usually black, drug dealers are often Hispanic, or white people are often rich. But in reality, there are many white people who are not rich, and there are criminals of every race. Many shows on television do not have any nonwhite characters. The same can be said of magazines. As a young black, Hispanic, or Asian male or female, you might feel less attractive or interesting because you do not see your race portrayed in the media.

Beauty Ideals

Young women who do not look like the so-called all-American beauty sometimes try to alter their appearance. Some try things as extreme as bleaching their skin or changing the shape of their eyes, nose, or body with plastic surgery. Every culture has different beauty standards.

For example, in Ethiopian culture, women with wide-set eyes and straight, distinct noses are considered beautiful. In other African cultures, women elongate their necks with elaborate neckpieces, and this, too, is considered beautiful. Ultimately, beauty has less to do with outward appearances and more to do with inner qualities, such as intelligence and a sense of humor. We can all work on appreciating people for their differences and admiring people not only physically, but also for their unique personalities.

Judging Others

You have probably heard the expression, "You can't judge a book by its cover." Yet, at the same time, all of us do judge books (i.e., people) by their covers, over and over again, and often unfairly. The first time you see someone, you are bound to form an impression of that person. A first impression is based on the surface details that you first observe—clothing (clean or dirty, fashionable or frumpy), hair (neat or messy, long or short), and also size, height, weight, and skin color. The problem is that an impression is never neutral. It is always, to a degree, negative or positive. It always involves making a judgment. The more different the person is, the more difficult it is to make a fair, unbiased, positive judgment.

If you have always lived in the same place and you always associate with people who are similar to you in

The media has a huge influence on people's opinions and attitudes and can indirectly contribute to racism.

terms of race, religion, ethnic background, and economic status, you might feel uncomfortable hanging out with someone who looks, speaks, dresses, or behaves differently. When you have never been exposed to different kinds of people, it is easy to make judgments based on stereotypes. Unfortunately, these stereotypes are often false. This is why you need to try and fight your tendency to judge someone based on a stereotype. Get to know a person as an individual before slotting him or her into a category. If you keep an open mind, you can react to a person based on who they are instead of who you think they are.

When Adam's uncle Lev invited him to go to the museum, Adam said yes, even though he wanted to say no. It wasn't that he didn't like hanging out with Lev. He did. At his house, though, in a mainly Jewish neighborhood, the sight of an Orthodox Jew dressed all in black was common.

The museum was in a different part of town. When Adam met his uncle in front of the subway, he caught some people looking at Lev strangely. Adam felt self-conscious and even angry with his uncle for being different. At the museum he purposefully kept his distance from Lev so that people would not stare at him, too. Later, when Adam got home, he felt rotten. It was not because he had not enjoyed the exhibit. But he had let what he imagined total strangers were thinking about him get in the way of him and his uncle having a good time together.

Like Adam, lots of teens are confronted with society's biases based solely on surface impressions. You or someone you know may have experienced situations similar to the following:

If I go into a fancy store with my white girl-friends, everything is cool. But if a week later, I go back by myself, I feel like I'm being watched. It's awful to be treated like a thief just for looking at a price tag.

— Raquel, Mexican, fifteen years old

Sometimes, when I'm on the subway with my buddies, we like to crack each other up. But some people—especially white ladies and white moms with little kids—will actually get up and sit somewhere else. It's like if you're a group of black guys making some noise, you're some dangerous gang or something.

— Jean, Haitian, sixteen years old

The kids at school think I'm dumb because I speak English with an accent. Some of them even imitate me. When we choose groups for presentations, nobody wants me in their group. They probably think I'm not as good as they are.

— Rajiv, Pakistani, fourteen years old

The guys I meet are always very into me when they find out I'm Brazilian. It's like they think I'm this easy party girl because I'm darker and from a tropical country. They treat me like I'm oversexed, and that's not who I am at all.

— Marta, Brazilian, seventeen years old

It was weird how my school guidance counselor kept pushing me to study computer science in college, even though I insisted that I wanted to go to acting school. Finally he told me to compare the

Fashion magazines show a very limited and unrealistic range of beauty.

The amount of exposure you have to people of different races depends greatly on where you live.

number of "Orientals" acting in films and on television with the number working in the computer industry.

— Damien, Taiwanese, eighteen years old

When situations such as these occur, you might be tempted to react in many different ways. What is the best way of dealing with such experiences? Is there one? To find out how to cope with, fight against, and overcome racial prejudice, keep reading.

Chapter Four

Dealing with Racism

In this chapter, you will find the practical advice of professionals and teens who have experienced racism and prejudice in many different situations.

Mina is fourteen years old. She is one of the few students of color at her new private school. Mina had attended public school for her whole life, and now she feels a little out of place. Most of her new classmates already know each other from their private junior high schools. Almost everyone lives in the area surrounding the school, which is a wealthy white neighborhood. Mina has to take an hour-and-a-half bus ride to school every morning from her working-class black neighborhood. At lunchtime she eats alone. The pretty and popular girls are the ones who are

skinny and blond. Being one of the only black stu-
dents in her classes makes Mina uncomfortable.
The worst is when they discuss slavery in history
class. It seems as if everyone thinks she knows
everything there is to know about black people and
black history. Mina sometimes wishes that she was
not so obviously different from her classmates.

It bothers her even more when her teachers don't
call on her at all. She is beginning to think her teach-
ers assume that because she is black she won't know
the answer. Mina has no idea whom to talk to about
this. She is thinking of asking her parents to let her
transfer to another school closer to home. When she
is in her neighborhood, she fits right in, but here
she feels very negative about herself.

Racism has had such a powerful effect that sometimes those who have suffered from it may try different
ways of dealing with it. Some people try to ignore it,
some try harder to fit in. Others may try to lose their
accent, change their hair, or deny that they like a certain
kind of food or music. These people deny their heritage
in an attempt to be accepted. Unfortunately, these ideas
about fitting in and being like everybody else are rein-
forced by many different people in our society.

In Mina's case, it was her teachers who were reinforcing
these negative ideas. Being one of the few students of
color at her school made her feel as if something was

wrong with her. Some of her teachers treated her differently. When a person says or does something racist to you, it can feel like a slap in the face. If it happens over and over, you might start to believe what you are being told.

If you are continually in situations where you feel that people have low expectations of you, you may begin to have low expectations for yourself and end up not caring at all. This can be the case if you do not already have a strong sense of self. For example, if your teacher assumes you do not know the answer and never calls on you, you may end up making no effort and not participating in class. You think your teacher doesn't care, so why should you?

These negative feelings can lead to anger, sadness, discouragement, or even overcompensation—trying desperately to fit in and prove the racist is wrong. These are very real and serious emotions that must be addressed. You may begin to feel hopeless when you realize that no matter what you do or how hard you work, others see only a negative stereotype of you. They do not see the individual. It can be hard to accept that some people will never change the way they think about you.

A Teacher's Advice

How can Mina cope with the racism she experiences in the classroom? Cassius Gil, a high school teacher in New York, has some suggestions. "When a student

Teachers can offer support and advice if you are feeling discouraged about the racism you see or experience.

comes to me with a complaint about a teacher being prejudiced, I ask questions first to make sure the teacher really is being racist and not just strict. Then, if I decide the student is right, I tell [him or her] that the only thing [he or she] can do is work twice as hard, so the teacher has to give a good grade."

Gil also suggests that students keep all of their class notes, test scores, and papers, so that if a teacher should grade them unfairly, they will be able to show proof of their work. Gil also says it is important to talk to other teachers who care about you or to the principal, so that they know what is going on before it becomes a problem. This way they have a record of complaints. If the situation persists, file a complaint with the school board.

There are ways for you to cope with the effects of racism without letting it destroy your faith in people or your self-confidence. One psychologist advises that you pick your battles. This is important because it is impossible to respond to everything all the time. You have only so much energy. If you try to fight every racist battle you encounter, you may be frustrated and angry a lot of the time. In some situations, it is important to speak up, but there are also other effective ways of dealing with racism that focus on making yourself stronger and more knowledgeable.

Know Your History

The best way to put things in perspective is to learn about your history. There are many books that can give you insight into what your community has gone through in order to survive (see the For Further Reading section at the end of this book). Learn why certain traditions are practiced. Knowing this type of information can help you if you ever decide to confront someone's bigoted remarks. Remember, often a person's prejudice is based on lack of knowledge.

Learn from Your Elders

Many of us come from communities that believe in respecting and cherishing our elders and our ancestors because they have lived through a lot. They can share a great deal of wisdom. Ask them about when they were children and about their lives. Hearing their stories may help you to see your family's successes and accomplishments.

Have Cultural Heroes

Think about how often you look to the movies for role models. Although there are positive celebrity role models, look around your community as well. There are sure to be people you admire for their courage or their commitment to something you find important. Find out about people in your community who are doing extraordinary things. Learn from them how they cope with stereotypes and still manage to be successful.

Find a Mentor

This is especially important if you are a minority at school or in your neighborhood. Sometimes it may seem that you are the only person going through a hard time. Talking to someone who is outside of your peer group is a good way to get support. Many schools, churches, and colleges have mentoring programs.

Understand That Race Isn't Always the Issue

Sometimes when you are Asian, Latino, Native North American, or African American, you may think that the only thing people notice about you is your race. Sometimes this is true, but not always. You would do yourself a disservice if you assumed that every time something bad happened to you it was because the

Responding to a racist remark isn't easy, but you may feel good about taking a stand.

other person was a racist. You might miss out on some valuable friendships. If you are always expecting racist treatment from other people, you may be creating problems where there aren't any.

Say Something

If someone makes a racist remark to you, you may decide it is best not to say anything. It can depend on your situation. But sometimes you may decide it is worth it to say something. It takes courage to speak your mind, but it can make you feel good to take a stand for something you believe in, whether or not the comment is directed at you. Here are some things you might try saying. A note of caution, however: If the person you are addressing is aggressive or angry, you should walk away and report the confrontation to an authority, especially if you are physically threatened.

"What you said was rude and disrespectful."
"I think you should apologize for saying that."

If the remark was not directed at you, you can still respond with the above statements, but you might add:

"I don't think those kinds of comments are funny."
"I think you should apologize to my friend."

Or you can always walk away.

Talk About It

It is always a good idea to talk through your feelings about racism. The most comfortable setting for this is among people who have been through the same thing; otherwise, you may find yourself teaching rather than sharing. Some high school and college campuses have cultural groups and classes that address issues of racism.

File a Report

You may decide to report an act of racism. If you are physically threatened or hurt, or if you feel you are being discriminated against on the job or at school, you may decide to take action. Speak to an adult about it first. He or she may be able to help you decide on a proper course of action. The first thing to do is write down what happened. Try to be as objective as you can when reporting the event. Use words that honestly describe the act. Write down where it happened and when it happened. Be as clear as possible. This will help your case if and when you go to court. Remember, filing a complaint isn't easy. However, if you feel strongly about what happened to you or someone else, take action.

Leo felt weird about going to the march his friend Brian had invited him to. Brian's whole family was going. The protesters were concerned about the increasing police violence against young black males in their community. Brian's eyes glinted angrily when he told Leo how in the last six months, four innocent black teens had been shot. Leo and Brian had played pickup basketball with one of the guys. He had seemed like a really good guy.

"We have nothing against you being friends with Brian," Leo's parents had explained to him. "But we don't like you spending time in that neighborhood."

Leo understood his parents' concern, but Brian was his close friend. It was for this reason that he had agreed to go to the march. But now he was having second thoughts. What if he was the only white guy to show up at the march? Wouldn't all the black marchers resent his presence? It was too late to chicken out now.

When Leo arrived at the park, he was surprised to see that not all of the protesters were black. And far from resenting his presence, the black people he met—friends and neighbors of Brian's family—seemed to genuinely appreciate his presence. The march wasn't angry or violent at all. Everybody sang peace songs and laughed and talked. Carrying a sign that read "Say No to Racial Violence" on it, Leo walked between Brian and his uncle Jake, who had marched on Washington with Martin Luther King.

"You know, Leo," said Jake when they arrived at City Hall. "It's great that you're here. Most folks think that violence against blacks or any other group is the problem of that group. But it's everybody's problem. And it takes everybody getting involved to make it better."

Chapter Five

Making a Difference

In this final chapter we will try to address the question of how you can stop the hate and prejudice you see around you. It starts with yourself. It would be wonderful if we could simply wish away racism and prejudice. But life is not that simple, and we all have a darker side that stereotypes people and judges them for the color of their skin. Overcoming our own prejudices is a part of our lives, whether we like it or not. But we can deal with that by being aware of our prejudices and working to overcome them. As we have seen in this book, racism can be a very complicated issue.

For example, according to the law, cabdrivers should not discriminate against their passengers. In many cities in the United States, however, cabdrivers refuse to pick up passengers because of their race. Some cabdrivers believe it is their right to refuse, saying that there is a higher possibility they will be robbed or physically threatened by certain passengers. But what about the person who cannot get a cab home at midnight no matter how many times he or she tries? The former mayor of New York City, David Dinkins (who is a black man), on one occasion could not get a cab to stop for him—even as the mayor of New York City! We must tell cabdrivers and all people who work in jobs that serve the people that they must perform their jobs. They cannot discriminate against people based on race.

Do Unto Others . . .

Once we have realized our own prejudices, we can try to build common bonds with people of all races. It is impossible to walk in another person's shoes (experience their life as they do), but that does not mean we should stop trying to understand each other. It is important to learn to empathize. That means trying to identify with other people. We also need to try to understand and be sensitive to their thoughts, experiences, and feelings.

When we experience prejudice directed at ourselves, we know it is unfair. It is also unfair when we do it to others. One of the most important steps in stopping racism is realizing that it is just as harmful when we are prejudiced toward others. The best way to bridge the distances and differences between "us" and "them" is to get to know each other. Sit down and

As you get to know people better, you often find that you have a lot in common.

talk. Instead of stereotyping individuals based on a whole group, get to know the person.

Change begins with one-to-one relationships. Once you get to know people who are different, you may still dislike some of them, but it will be for individual traits, not because of the color of their skin or the clothes they wear. Once you get to know an individual and learn about what makes him or her unique, then you can find things in common. When you treat all people with respect, others will treat you in the same manner. When you treat others with hatred and fear, they may do the same to you.

Sometimes it may seem that racism and prejudice will never be completely erased from our society. Many of you have probably felt that there was nothing you could do. You may not be able to enlighten people who do not want to change their racist attitudes. However, you do have power, and you can change your own attitudes. That is how you begin to make a difference in our society.

We suggested some ways of coping with racism in the last chapter. Those suggestions were meant as advice on how to keep racism and prejudice from hurting. Following are some important steps to take toward changing your own attitudes and the attitudes of others about racism and prejudice.

If you are neutral in situations of injustice, you have chosen the side of the oppressor.
—Desmond Tutu, Archbishop Emeritus of South Africa

Confront

When it is appropriate and when you feel safe and comfortable doing so, confront the forms of hatred, racism, and prejudice that you encounter. This means addressing racism in your family, friends, coworkers, and yourself. Monitor your own thoughts and feelings. When you think negatively of another person or group of people, ask yourself what those thoughts are based on. Are your thoughts based on feelings or facts? No racial slurs should be acceptable. Language is a powerful tool of hatred. Think about how horrible some racial slurs

If you feel comfortable, confront racism even if it comes from a friend and is not directed at you.

sound, then think about how much worse it must feel to be called those words.

Recognize Similarities

We are all individuals, and inevitably we have differences. But remember that we also share many traits and feelings. For example, no one wants to be rejected by others. We are all hurt by prejudice and racism. Ultimately, everyone wants to be understood. These are common bonds that can connect people of all races.

Accept

Taking pride in your own heritage does not make you a racist. It is also important, however, to accept people's differences. You can appreciate who you are and still have room to appreciate other kinds of people. This is not an easy thing to do. Even when you try to accept other people, you may clash in your ideas and opinions. It is impossible to like everyone we meet, but we should all try to be more tolerant of other cultures and lifestyles. North America is becoming more and more diversified. It is in everyone's best interest to accept others. Diversity is a positive thing, and one you can learn from.

Volunteer

Make an effort to volunteer and perform community service. Volunteering helps to bridge racial and cultural divisions. It can expose you to people with different life experiences from your own. It will also make you feel good to be contributing to the community. You can find places to volunteer through public listings in your local newspaper, at the public library's bulletin board, and through your place of worship. You may want to check your high school's counseling department. You may also want to work with children to help them learn about these issues.

Keep an Open Mind

Try to have an open mind about all people and experiences. Try to see people for who they are, not how they look. You must make an effort. We are all comfortable with what we are used to, but if you want to broaden your horizons, it is important to get out of your comfort zone and meet different people.

Having a diverse circle of friends can be a very enriching experience.

Consider joining a group that promotes interaction among people of different races. There may be a group in your community that already does this. If not, start your own group. Then when you do get together with a person of another race, look for things that you have in common. Focus on the similarities, not the differences.

Take a Stand in the Fight Against Racism

While you are trying to change your own ideas and those in your community, you can extend the fight against racism even further. Remember how much the media can foster stereotypes? Pay attention to what you watch on television and what you read in the newspapers. If you do not like something you see or read, write a letter. The media and their advertisers consider you a valuable consumer. They will listen to what you have to say. Let them know when they are contributing to racist attitudes and stereotypes. Remember: YOU do not have to experience racism yourself to fight against it.

These may seem like small efforts, but every effort that you make—big or small—is a step in the right direction.

Glossary

abolitionist in the 1800s, a person who fought to
end slavery.

assassinate To murder by sudden or secret attack,
usually for political reasons.

bigotry Acts and beliefs of a person who strongly
holds on to his or her intolerance and prejudice.

boycott To refuse to deal with a person, store, or
organization as a way to express disapproval or
force them to accept certain conditions.

discrimination Treating someone differently for
reasons other than individual merit, such as race,
gender, class, or religion.

diverse Having different elements; varied.

empathize To understand and be sensitive to
another's thoughts and feelings without actually
having those thoughts or feelings.

enlighten To give knowledge or to instruct.

heritage Culture and traditions that are handed down from previous generations.

ignorance Lack of knowledge.

immigration Entry into another country to live.

intimidate To influence by fear.

persecution Mistreatment of a person because of his or her beliefs.

prejudice Judgment or opinion of someone or something without adequate knowledge.

segregation The separation of people of different races in schools, restaurants, hospitals, and other such places.

stereotype An oversimplified opinion of a group of people based on general or limited information.

unconstitutional Not allowed by the Constitution of the United States.

white supremacy The belief that white people are superior to all other races.

Where to Go for Help

In the United States

American Civil Liberties Union (ACLU)
The national ACLU suggests you check your local phone book for the number of the office near you.
http://www.aclu.org

Anti-Defamation League
823 United Nations Plaza
New York, NY 10017
(212) 885-7700
http://www.adl.org
This group defends Jewish people while working to seek justice and fair treatment for all people.

Community Cousins
140 Encinitas Boulevard
Suite 220

Encinitas, CA 92024
(619) 944-CUZZ.
http://groupweb.com/cc/cousins.htm
This nonprofit group matches individuals and families of different backgrounds. They can help you start a group in your community. Call for a free manual.

HateWatch

HateWatch monitors hate group activity on the Internet. Groups are listed by category and country.
http://www.hatewatch.org

In Canada

Artists Against Racism

Box 54511
Toronto, ON M5M 4N5
(416) 410-5631
http://www.vrx.net/aar/
This nonprofit organization uses youth idols such as musicians and actors to help teens combat prejudice.

Canadian Ethnocultural Council (CEC)

251 Laurier Avenue West, Suite 1100
Ottawa, ON K1P 5J6
(613) 230-3867

http://www.web.net/~cec/
A nonprofit umbrella organization for groups that deal with racism, ethnoculturalism, minority, and new immigrant issues.

Canadian Race Relations Foundation (CRRF)
4900 Yonge Street, Suite 1305
Willowdale, ON M2N 6A4
(888) 240-4936/(416) 952-3500
http://www.crr.ca/
A group that works to combat racism and all forms of racial discrimination in Canada.

Equality Today
E-zine with articles about racism written by young people.
http://www.equalitytoday.org/

For Further Reading

Bernier-Grand, Carmen T. *In the Shade of the Nispero Tree*. New York: Orchard Books, 1999.

Birdseye, Debbie Holsclaw. *Under Our Skin: Kids Talk About Race*. New York: Holiday House, 1997.

Cooper, Michael L. *The Double V Campaign: African Americans and World War II*. New York: Lodestar Books, 1998.

Fisher, Leonard Everett. *To Bigotry No Sanction: The Story of the Oldest Synagogue in America*. New York: Holiday House, 1999.

Fremon, David K. *Japanese-American Internment in American History*. Springfield, NJ: Enslow Publishers, 1996.

Gillam, Scott. *Discrimination: Prejudice in Action*. Springfield, NJ: Enslow Publishers, 1995.

Guernsey, Joann Bren. *Affirmative Action: A Problem or a Remedy?* Minneapolis, MN: Lerner

Publications, 1997.

Lynch, Chris. *Mick*. New York: HarperCollins, 1996.

Muse, Daphne, ed. *Prejudice: Stories About Hate, Ignorance, Revelation and Transformation*. New York: Hyperion, 1998.

Myers, Walter Dean. *The Journal of Joshua Loper: A Black Cowboy*. New York: Scholastic, 1999.

Staples, Suzanne Fisher. *Dangerous Skies*. New York: HarperTrophy, 1998.

Index

Index

About the Author

Nasoan Sheftel-Gomes is a freelance writer living in New York City. She has a BA from Clark University in sociology and women's studies and a master's of journalism from the University of California at Berkeley. Nasoan grew up in San Francisco, the child of a Jewish-American mother and an African-American/Cape-Verdean father.

Photo Credits

Cover photo by Reuters/Jeff Christensen/Archive Photos; pp. 10, 14, 18 by Photoworld/FPG International; p. 13 by Archive Photos; p. 16 by Express Newspapers/H392/Archive Photos; p. 22 by AP/Wide World Photos; p. 25 by FPG International; all other photos by Ira Fox.